POP ART

Christian Demilly

Pop Art

"Popular, transient, low cost, mass produced, young, witty, sexy, gimmicky, glamourous, big business."

RICHARD HAMILTON

Prestel

Munich · Berlin · London · New York

"THE GREATEST ENEMY OF ART IS GOOD TASTE"

Marcel Duchamp

In 1917, the French artist Marcel Duchamp put a urinal in an exhibition in New York. He signed his "piece" with a name he made up: R. Mutt. From 1918 onward, the German artist Kurt Schwitters started to make collages using all sorts of things he had collected, such as advertisements, newspaper cuttings, and tram tickets. At the same period in Paris, the artist Fernand Léger was painting scenes of industrial society, covering large areas in primary colors. But what has Pop Art got to do with this?

What is now seen as a typically American art movement was in fact originally inspired by European artists forty years earlier.

Like Duchamp, Pop Art went on to transform ordinary daily objects into works of art. Like Kurt Schwitters, Pop Art made use of bits and pieces from everyday life, which were put together and turned into works of art. Like Fernand Léger, Pop Art was to develop into a reflection of society at that time, often presented in a rather mechanical way.

2   **Kurt Schwitters, *En Morn*, 1947**

Fernand Léger, *Disks in the City*, 1920

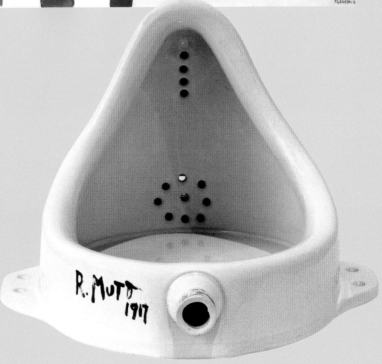

Marcel Duchamp, *Fountain*, 1917/1964

Richard Hamilton, *Just what is it that makes today's homes so different, so appealing?*, 1956

HOME *Sweet* HOME

After the Second World War, America's influence on the rest of the world became increasingly strong. Much of Europe lay in ruins, and everything had to be rebuilt. Meanwhile, America was doing well. Consumer goods, daily comforts, a feeling of well-being, and ample leisure time—these were the things that formed "The American Way of Life," and Europe soon followed suit. Chewing gum, Coca-Cola, and American cigarettes all become familiar on the European continent. America not only exported its products and value system, but also its culture: Films, cartoons, television, music—a culture popular with the masses. In England, a number of artists watched this influence growing, and with a certain fascination and some irony they gave some thought to these images of happiness promised to them by modern comforts: The perfect body, vacuum cleaners to make life easier, canned food, and comfy sofas. All of these things are to be found in Richard Hamilton's collage of 1956, including signs of a culture "made in the USA"—a cinema, posters, comic-style stories about love and romance, and advertisements. Eduardo Paolozzi also used this imagery and even included the famous Coca-Cola logo in his work shown above. And in both these collages, a little word can be seen—a simple little word: Pop!

"Paintings look more like real life if they are composed from the elements of real life" ROBERT RAUSCHENBERG

America has always been a country surrounded by myths. These myths were turned into images which all Americans could identify with. They were strong images that documented the great events of American history, as well as everyday life. Movies showed the conquest of the Wild West, and posters boasted technological progress and economic prosperity. Using movies, advertisements, and art, America put itself in the limelight and held up a mirror to itself. We are all familiar with these images,

and whether we want to or not, they are all food for our imagination: Cowboys riding across enless plains, gas stations and motels on deserted roads, or the conquest of space. Pop artists also seized on these images of America, collected them, and made them their primary source of inspiration. And as America was the focus of the western world during the 1960s, artists who concentrated on America, were documenting society as a whole.

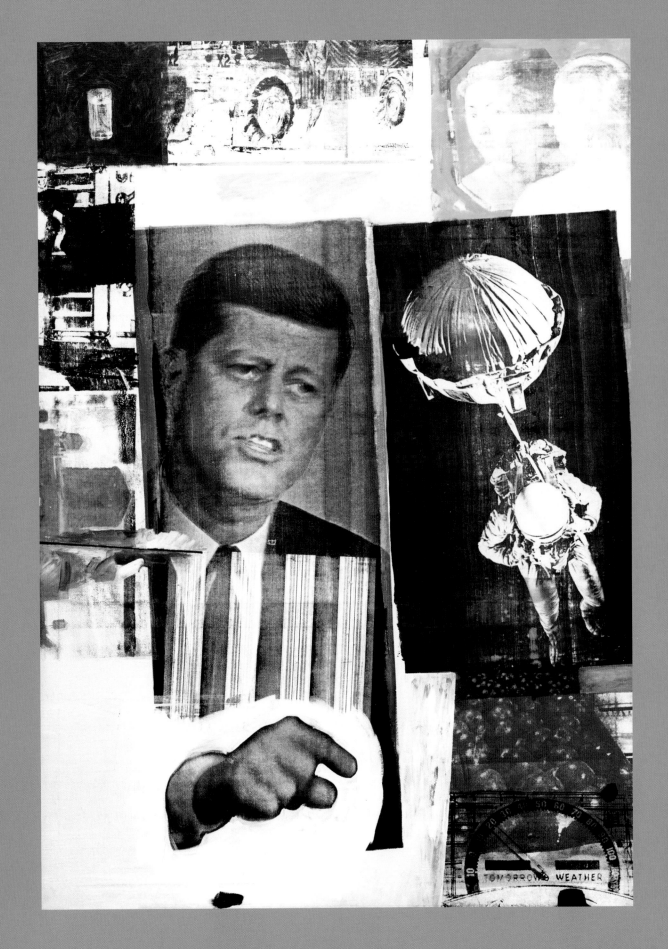

Robert Rauschenberg, *Retroactive II*, 1964

POWER OPPORTUNITIES PEOPLE

Edward Ruscha, *Large Trademark with Eight Spotlights*, 1962

Pop! That's the sound of a bottle of champagne being opened. Bubbles, glitter, and sequins—these are all symbolic of America in the 1960s. The world of the cinema, film stars, and money; it was a fascinating world! Pop Art reflects America's glamorous image like a mirror. It documents the whole world's obsession with the lights of Hollywood, and with the smiles of Marilyn Monroe or Liz Taylor. American films developed into a mass culture, and its stars become idols, known and admired throughout the world. They were fabricated images which encouraged our dreams and touched us on an emotional level. Like popular magazines, Pop Art clamors for our attention, showing us luxury which is inaccessible, a waste of time, and superficial. These are the images that reached the masses. But after all, what is art? Images, simply images, and nothing but images.

Andy Warhol, *80 Two Dollar Bills*, 1962 9

The Hidden Face
of America

Pop! This is also the sound of a gun fitted with a silencer. Sometimes the reality behind the pleasant facade is more serious and less amusing. The mirror produced by Pop Artists wasn't always so glamourous. America has different faces—the electric chair, the bomb dropped on Hiroshima, violence, and poverty. America is fascinating but can also be a frightening place. Pop artists also showed this other more disturbing side. But they didn't pass judgement, they just reproduced what they saw and put it on display. Here again, they used images with which we are all familiar, and transformed them into static works of art. We can still see such images in quick succession in magazines and on television. We are exposed to so many pictures that they become meaningless, and in the end we forget them.

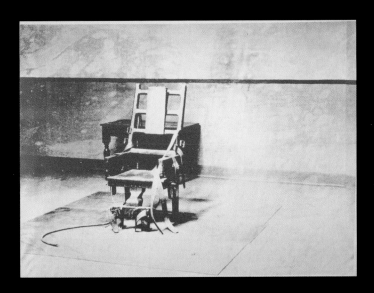

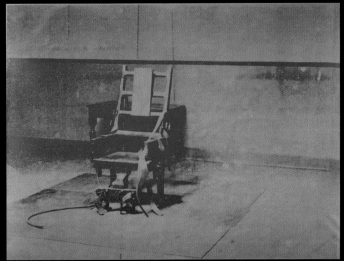

Pop artists immortalised such pictures on canvas, so that no one could forget them. Like artists before them who were commissioned to paint portraits of important people so that they could take their place in history, Pop artists offer us a portrait of America, a portrait of society, without giving an opinion. They leave the decisions to us.

Andy Warhol, *Electric Chair*, 1967

Andy Warhol, *Electric Chair*, 1967

Claes Oldenburg, *Pepsi-Cola Sign*, 1961

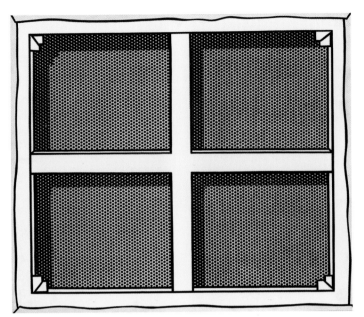

Art? DID YOU SAY Art?

For a long time, art had been synonymous with great technical mastery and invention. Artists were familiar with all techniques relevant to painting and sculpture, using every pencil, brush or chisel with characteristic ease. Artists were also people who—out of practically nothing—invented or created universes and images which had never existed before. Whereas artists have long drawn on noble themes such as religion, mythology, nature, or important people as a source of inspiration, Pop Art broke all boundaries and mixed genres. Pop artists were inspired by the humdrum routine of daily life—by objects as meaningless as a can of soup, for example. They made use of things that already existed, like posters, photographs, dollar bills, newspaper articles, or boxes of detergent, which they mixed together, reassembled, reproduced, or used however they wished. Their methods were actually more like those used by advertising agencies or graphic artists. Andy Warhol, for example, often used the technique of silk-screen printing which enabled him to produce a whole series of images by putting one layer of ink on another in a variety of colors. Several famous names in Pop art had had other jobs before becoming artists, such as in advertising, graphic art, or design.
So, is this really "art"?

Pop Art can laugh at itself and often shows us the secret of how a work of art is produced. The act of painting is not important. In this work by Roy Lichtenstein, the canvas has been turned around, encouraging the viewer to appreciate art from behind.

Andy Warhol, *Flowers II*, 1964

Roy Lichtenstein, *Stretcher Frame with Cross Bars III*, 1968

13

LAUGHING AT ART

Pop Art is a mirror of society. But sometimes it is a distorted mirror. Even if it does nothing more than present us with an object, it still chooses what to show us, and it obviously has reasons for making certain choices. Hamburgers are nothing extraordinary: They are part of our life, and millions of people eat them every day without thinking twice.

But if a hamburger suddenly turns into a huge, soft sculpture, it suddenly takes on a whole new dimension. It's really quite funny. Here, Pop Art reflects a consumer society which always wants more. It points its finger at the reality of our society, including its excesses. Pop Art has a laugh at the things and the images with which we surround ourselves on

a daily basis. In advertisements and in the media, images of women are everywhere and in constant use: Sexy and glamourous, pretty girls with dazzling smiles sell us toothpaste, margarine, happiness, and dreams. Mel Ramos had fun with this, as shown in his picture of a young naked starlet reclining on a huge pat of cheese spread. With this image, which makes us think of American comics or circus posters, he parodied ancient sculptures reclining on pedestals. Pop Art plays with stereotypes— images which have been seen and seen again, images so familiar that we are no longer aware of them. This is another of art's intentions: To make us see objects which no longer attract our attention, and to laugh at them!

Claes Oldenburg, *Floor Burger*, 1962 15

"In objects I discover society, and in objects society discovers itself as well"
CLAES OLDENBURG

Art is supposed to touch us, to move us, and to show us something beautiful or unique. But is a can of soup or a light switch beautiful? Can we be touched by a glass of whiskey presented in a cold, neutral style? What can this art convey to us about objects which we already know inside out? Why did Pop artists choose to hide behind the images they showed us, as if these could have been produced by anyone? Perhaps, quite simply, they were drawing our attention to the beauty of everyday things? Our daily routine is nothing more than a combination of thousands

James Rosenquist, *Glass of Whiskey*, 1969

Andy Warhol, *Campbell's Soup Can I*, 1969

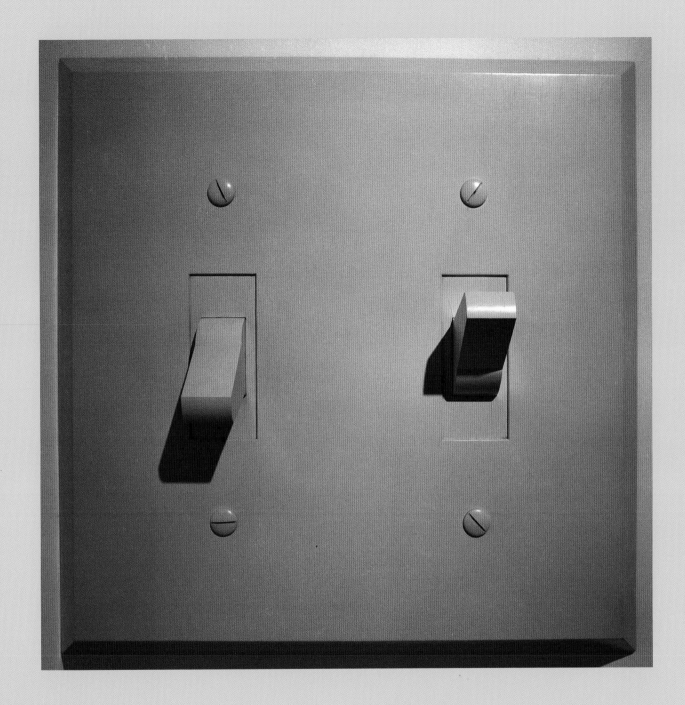

of rare and exceptional moments; it consists of thousands of repeated gestures, thousands of little insignificant things. We are intimately connected through these daily actions. When we switch on a light, perhaps the neighbor next door or someone on the other side of the world is doing exactly the same. Our gestures are individual but simultaneously universal. In their own way, Pop artists inform us about ourselves and about the world as a whole.

Claes Oldenburg, *Light Switches—Hard Version*, 1964

Tom Wesselmann, *Still Life*, **1962**

"Everyone looks and acts alike"
ANDY WARHOL

Pop Art uses unspectacular methods to present us a world which we all have in common. This is a world inhabited by Mr. and Mrs. Average. Objects are interchangeable. Mass production results in a standardized universe. No matter where in the world we are, we have the same points of reference: Everyone has drunk Coca-Cola, everyone has heard of Hollywood, and everyone knows fast food. Andy Warhol, one of Pop Art's greatest figures, said: "The extraordinary thing about America is that it is the first country to inaugurate a system in which the richest consumers actually buy the same things as the poorest consumers. When you see a televised advertisement for Coca-Cola, you realise that the president is drinking Coca-Cola, Liz Taylor is drinking Cola-Cola and—amazingly—you are also drinking Coca-Cola. Coca-Cola is simply Coca-Cola, and no money in the world can buy you a better quality of Coca-Cola than the one being drunk by the drifter on the corner of the street. Whatever sort of Coca-Cola it is, it is bound to be good. Liz Taylor knows it, the president knows it, and you know it too."

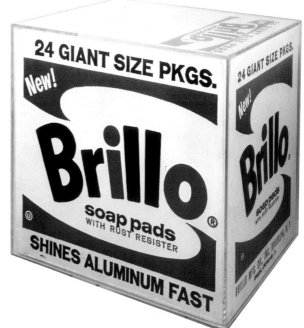

"BIG STORES ARE A BIT LIKE MUSEUMS"
Andy Warhol

The America of the 1960s was a society of mass consumerism. What does that mean? It means that this prosperous society produced an increasingly large number of objects in huge quantities—aerosols, television aerials, cars, canned food, cornflakes, fridges, vacuum cleaners, and washing machines—for an ever-increasing number of consumers. Advertisements showed how happiness came from consumerism and possessions. Society no longer suggested but imposed; it insisted that you had enough money to access modern happiness, to avoid getting stuck

on the sidelines. Pop Art was a processing movement. It was on the receiving end of society: It received inspiration from society and collected everything it produced because all the products indicated the nature of that society. Pop artists were not living in an ivory tower: They understood the system and used it to their advantage. Is society a consumer society? In this case, Pop Art is also consumer art, art which is "popular, transient, low cost, mass produced, young, witty, sexy, gimmicky, glamourous, big business." (Richard Hamilton)

Andy Warhol, *Brillo*, 1964

James Rosenquist, *I love you with my Ford,* **1961**

22   **The Beatles, record cover for** *Sgt. Pepper's Lonely Hearts Club Band*, **1967**

POP Culture

Pop Art was interested in everything which enjoyed popularity: Films, film stars, advertising, cars, or other objects. But Pop Art itself became popular. It was inspired by music, graphic art and design, and in turn, it influenced music, graphic art, and design. Pop Art wanted to break down the barriers between these genres, between major and lesser art, between the elevated and the ordinary. In America and in England, the 1960s turned into an incredible cultural melting pot. The arts started to mix, and cartoons and pop music turned into art forms of their own. Pop became synonymous with color, fantasy, humor, and glamour. It was also synonymous with an alternative culture. On the record cover of their album *Sgt. Pepper's Lonely Hearts Club Band*, the Beatles posed in flamboyant suits before a crowd of celebrities (actors, sportsmen, and writers), who they selected themselves, and as such created their own "celebrity museum." This record cover was designed by Peter Blake, an English Pop Artist. Andy Warhol designed the record cover for the first album recorded by the New York band, The Velvet Underground, which he supported. Art, music, stars, popular culture—everything was alive, on the move, and intermingling. That's Pop!

Andy Warhol, cover for the album *The Velvet Underground and Nico*, 1967

MEANWHILE, IN EUROPE ...

Pop Art, originally influenced by European artists, later became a source of inspiration for European art, too. The spirit of Pop Art was enthusiastically adopted in England, Germany, and France: Changing, reproducing, and playing with well-known images, and demonstrating a strong interest in "reality" in the form of objects. During the 1960s, many artists immersed themselves in this genre. In the work on the right dated 1964, the artist Alain Jacquet was inspired by a famous painting by Édouard Manet from 1863. In order to parody this, Alain Jacquet used techniques which were typical of Pop Art: A photograph was taken and

reproduced as a silk screen print on such a large scale that we can see the individual dots —the blue, red, yellow, and black blobs of color that make up the photo. In this way, a famous French painting was turned into a Pop Art poster! In *Suddenly Last Summer*, Martial Raysse took the photograph of a woman who appeared in an advertisement for sun cream as the basis for his work, and created a mixture of painting, photography, and sculpture. The photograph was enlarged and painted over, and a real hat and scarf was added to the foreground. This ordinary, anonymous image suddenly evokes a world of poetry, nostalgia, and emotion.

Alain Jacquet, *Le Déjeuner sur l'herbe,* **1964**

Now playing,
AT A CINEMA NEAR YOU !

Pop! Popular art, depicting daily life: The objects we use every day made their debut in the world of "official" art; art moved closer to the public and become part of its daily existence. In the 1980s, American artists took things into their own hands: Keith Haring, a cartoon and graffiti artist, decided to show his work in the New York Subway. He brought art to the streets, showing all his work in simple forms and clear colors. At the same time he commercialized his figures in different media by creating posters, T-shirts, and postcards, because art is also a commercial commodity. The American artist Jeff Koons was more than aware of this, too. From the 1980s onward, he collected objects often considered too ordinary or in bad taste (china dogs, inflatable toys, and ornaments) and transformed them into objects of art. His brightly colored works are inspired by advertising, a consumer society, and popular imagery, just like the work shown here in which the famous pink panther is seen arm in arm with a blonde pin-up girl.

Jeff Koons, *Pink Panther,* **1988**

Keith Haring, *Untitled,* **1989**

"I TAKE A CLICHÉ AND TRY TO ORGANIZE ITS FORMS TO MAKE IT MONUMENTAL"
Roy Lichtenstein

Pop Art was originally inspired by European art, and first emerged in England in the 1950s, althought it only really took off in America in the 1960s. Everything which was then new—culture and mass consumption, huge supermarkets, modern comforts—is now part of our daily lives. Television is everywhere, everyone goes shopping in supermarkets and eats at fast food restaurants. More than ever before, we dream of money and film stars. Half fascinated and half revolted by this, Pop artists played a major role in the birth of a new society, showing us the power of an America capable of changing the direction of the world. Pop Art attempts to show us the positive side but also the excesses of society. Through their images, artists presented us with a world where images themselves were increasingly significant. They made use of objects to represent a society full of objects. Pop Art is full of life, it is reactive, and dynamic. It is an art genre which is anchored in reality, in the most astonishing and the most ordinary of things—a reality which is simply human. We can accept or reject the world as we please. We can criticise it or admire it. Pop Art invites us just to face it with a certain measure of detachment and irony, with fantasy and cheer: The cheerful face of Pop Art!

Roy Lichtenstein, *Girl with a Ball*, 1961

Biographies

JASPER JOHNS (BORN 1930)

Together with Robert Rauschenberg, Jasper Johns is one of the main precursors of Pop Art. He studied at the University of South Carolina before completing his first stint in New York as a commercial artist. He and Robert Rauschenberg become good friends, and gradually Johns moved away from the world of commercial art so that he could dedicate himself to painting. He immediately started focusing on American symbols by depicting whole series of American flags, dollars, and targets. When Johns chose the American flag as a motif for his work, he did not necessarily choose it as a symbol of the federal unity of the American people, for the Cold War had taken its toll, and Vietnam was just around the corner. He is enigmatic, and exploits it as if it is a simple element detached from any particular significance or identity.

ROY LICHTENSTEIN (1923-97)

After studying art in New York, Roy Lichtenstein was very inspired by Cubism and Abstract Expressionism, a pictorial movement led by painters such as Jackson Pollock and Mark Rothko. During the Second World War, he enrolled in the American army, and later this experience propelled him to produce works which center on the violence of war. But the style characteristic to most of his paintings did not crystallize until 1961. His sources of inspiration were images of mass consumerism, such as cartoons or advertisements. But he did not attempt to raise these modes of expression to the level of art: He readjusted and reproduced them on huge canvasses so that the spectator receives a shock on a grand and graphic scale. In a similar way, Lichtenstein modified works by great painters such as Pablo Picasso, Henri Matisse, Franz Marc, or Claude Monet. Here too, he expanded, distorted, and altered the subjects of paintings which inspired him.

Roy Lichtenstein, *In the Car*, 1963

RICHARD HAMILTON (BORN 1922)

Richard Hamilton is the founder and the best-known representative of English Pop Art. He took evening classes at the Royal Academy in London while working in advertising and design. His early work was strongly influenced by abstract art and Cubism. But in 1956, at a group exhibition, he presented a work consisting of collages, like the Dada artists, using photographs taken from magazines. Here, on a giant lollipop held by a body-builder, the word POP can be seen. For many, this marks the beginning of the Pop Art movement. After meeting Pop artists in New York in 1963, he integrated different materials in his work. This universally recognised artist later organised exhibitions together with Eduardo Paolozzi (friend and confidant of Marcel Duchamp) who taught at the Royal College of Art in London.

CLAES OLDENBURG (BORN 1929)

Swedish by origin, Claes Oldenburg studied at Yale University, then signed up for courses at the Chicago Art Institute, before he settled in New York in 1956. He was influenced by Art Brut and his first works were created from materials which he had collected: Pieces of plastic or paper which he had picked up on the streets. He produced figures in plaster that he exhibited and sold in his studio, which was managed like a boutique. His intention was to undermine the traditional structure of the art market by offering his works directly to the consumer. In 1962 he exhibited his soft sculptures, which completely transformed the objects represented as a result of the scale and the material. Examples of these are his cloth basin, or his giant hamburger made of sponge and plastic. He took this even further when he constructed huge models of tiny objects, such as lipstick or a shuttlecock, so that they assume an absurd or grotesque appearance.

MEL RAMOS (BORN 1935)

Together with Edward Ruscha, Mel Ramos is one of Pop Art's painters from the west coast of the United States. He studied art in Sacramento, California. Ramos's work is very individual. One of his favorite subjects is the half-clad pin-up girl so often found in advertisements for cars or suntan lotion. Photographs served as his source of inspiration, which he then transformed, raising them to the level of art. However, both Andy Warhol and Mel Ramos found inspiration for their art anywhere and everywhere. A tin of soup is just as good as an advertisement in a magazine. When he composes his paintings he introduces aspects of the absurd, or incongruous elements, for example a pin-up girl riding a hippopotamus or sitting comfortably on a huge hamburger. When people react with astonishment he simply says: "I am for an art that attacks the eyes, I love sight thrills."

ROBERT RAUSCHENBERG (BORN 1925)

Together with Jasper Johns, Robert Rauschenberg is considered one of the precursors of Pop Art. After studying art at the Kansas City Institute, he spent some time in Paris to complete his studies. There he was influenced by the contemporary art trends of the period, and produced huge abstract paintings. He did not hesitate to include other elements into his paintings, such as newspaper cuttings or pieces of material, similar in style to the collages of the Dada movement. In the course of integrating more and more material and objects, his work became a hybrid between painting and sculpture. In this way he attempted to influence the viewer, even issuing warnings by integrating road signs or car number plates into his works.

JAMES ROSENQUIST (BORN 1933)

Having completed his studies at art school in New York, James Rosenquist worked as a stylist creating public signs. But Robert Rauschenberg and Jasper Johns encouraged him to turn to painting, and he started to produce abstract works. From 1960 onward, he became an important representative of Pop Art, painting very large canvases concentrating on themes taken from advertising. He rearranged very colorful but unrelated subjects on a single canvas, for example a bowl of noodles and a car, but with this juxtaposition of diverse elements his intention was to denounce mass consumerism. His work is also very political when for example illustrating the media hype surrounding American presidents, the fleeting power of film stars, or the threat of nuclear armament.

EDWARD RUSCHA (BORN 1937)

When Edward Ruscha signed up for art school in Los Angeles, he took courses in graphic art and commercial drawing. But his encounter with the work of Jaspar Johns left him reeling. He changed his orientation and turned towards art. Like Andy Warhol, he never actually detached himself fully from the style of his initial training, but his work became more lyrical, for example in his depictions of an isolated gas station, an endless road, or the landscape of American suburbia. Los Angeles is also a major source of inspiration for him—not only visually as a city, but also as home of the myth-producing film industry. He does not portray film stars, but rather the signs and logos of film companies which are immediately identifiable. Words and phrases play an essential role in Ruscha's work. He uses text carefully and lends it a certain force so that it becomes a formidable force, and almost lets it speak for itself.

ANDY WARHOL (1928-87)

The son of Czech immigrants, Andy Warhol was a quiet child who spent a lot of time reading comics. He used to collect photographs of the film stars of the era, who he had seen in the cinema. His fascination for pictorial images impelled him to start studying decoration and commercial art in Pittsburgh in the United States. But New York attracted him more, and there he quickly found success as an illustrator for various magazines. In 1962 he exhibited his first silk-screen prints (the *Campbell Soup* and *Two Dollar Bill* series) which represented his first steps in the art world. For Warhol, the process of silk-screen printing becomes an extremely important technique, but he was also interested in other media such as photography, film, and music. He even worked as producer for a rock group. A symbol of the New York art scene, Andy Warhol moved to an abandoned factory and created "The Art Factory." This developed into a significant meeting place for actors, painters, and musicians.

TOM WESSELMANN (1931-2004)

Two years after finishing at the Cooper Union School of Art in New York, Tom Wesselmann enjoyed great success with his exhibition "The Great American Nude" in 1961. He showed a series of female nudes, the composition of which was greatly inspired by Henri Matisse. They depict women reclining casually against very colorful oriental backgrounds. From then onward, he explored all contours of the female body, sometimes placing it in a provocative pose, and sometimes presenting it as a silhouette or simply as a face dominated by a large, red, sensual mouth as in some advertisements. To make his models more lifelike, he did not hesitate to show them in his decorative pieces, paintings, installations, and sculptures doing banal household chores. But despite all the glamour, Tom Wesselmann simultaneously pointed an accusing finger at a consumer society which glorifies appearances and fleeting youth.

© Prestel Verlag, Munich · Berlin · London · New York 2007
© for the original French edition: Éditions Palette..., Paris 2006

The title and concept of the "Adventures in Art" series and
the titles and design of its individual volumes are protected
by copyright and may not be copied or imitated in any way.

Prestel books are available worldwide. Please contact your
nearest bookseller of one of the following addresses for
information concerning your local distributor.

Prestel Verlag
Königinstrasse 9
80539 Munich
Tel. +49 (89) 38 17 09-0
Fax +49 (89) 38 17 09-35

Prestel Publishing Ltd.
4 Bloomsbury Place
London WC1A 2QA
Tel. +44 (0) 20 7323-5004
Fax +44 (0) 20 7636-8004

Prestel Publishing
900 Broadway. Suite 603
New York, N.Y. 10003
Tel. +1 (212) 995-2720
Fax +1 (212) 995-2733

www.prestel.com

Library of Congress Control Number: 2007928842

British Library Cataloguing-in-Publication Data: a catalogue
record for this book is available from the British Library
The Deutsche Bibliothek holds a record of this publication
in the Deutsche Nationalbibliografie; detailed bibliographical
data can be found under: http://dnb.ddb.de

Translated from the French by Rosie Jackson, Munich
Copyedited by Christopher Wynne, Munich
Design by Loïc Le Gall

Printed in Italy on acid-free paper

ISBN 978-3-7913-3894-1